The Old-Time Radio Trivia Book II

ALSO BY MEL SIMONS:

The Old-Time Radio Trivia Book

The Old-Time Television Trivia Book

Old-Time Radio Memories

The Show-Biz Trivia Book

Old-Time Television Memories

The Movie Trivia Book

Voices from the Philco

The Good Music Trivia Book

The Mel Simons Joke Book: If It's Laughter You're After

The Old-Time Radio Trivia Book II

by Mel Simons

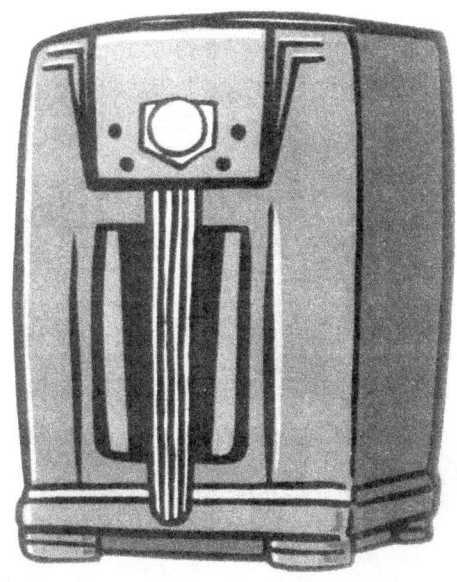

BearManor Media
2013

The Old-Time Radio Trivia Book II

© 2013 Mel Simons

All rights reserved.

For information, address:

BearManor Media
P. O. Box 71426
Albany, GA 31708

bearmanormedia.com

Typesetting and layout by John Teehan

Published in the USA by BearManor Media

ISBN — 1-59393-744-X
978-1-59393-744-7

Dedication

*This book is dedicated to my grandniece,
Liv Goldman*

Mel Simons
www.melsimons.net

A  OF THANKS

A special thank you to Tony King. In addition to doing my website, Tony finds many terrific things for me on the computer. Not only is Tony a computer genius, he has become a super friend.

Bob Hastings and Mel Simons

Foreword

When I recently ran into Mel at an "Old-Time Radio" convention in Cincinnati, Ohio, we talked fondly about the "good old days" of radio. He seemed to know more about Archie, Betty, Veronica, Reggie, and Jughead than I did; and I'm the guy who was the voice of Archie Andrews for eight years (1946-1954) on NBC Radio.

Mel's knowledge of the "Golden Days of Radio" stems from his childhood love of radio shows to his vast collection of old-time radio memorabilia to his personal friendships with the people who made the characters come alive—among them Bob Elliott (*Bob and Ray*), Julie Stevens (*The Romance of Helen Trent*), Ezra Stone (*The Aldrich Family*), and Brett Morrison (*The Shadow*).

This book, *The Old-Time Radio Trivia Book II*—the tenth in Mel's "nostalgia" series—once again gives you the chance to test your knowledge of the shows you too loved on mid-twentieth-century radio, and while doing so will make you smile and laugh out loud as you warmly remember a time before the clutter of computers, smart phones, and iPads. Let's go back to radio and use our imaginations. Much better than the junk on TV.

– Bob Hastings
Radio's Archie Andrews

Jack Benny

Quiz #1

JACK BENNY

(Answers on page 109)

1. What was Jack's theme song?
2. Who played Mr. Kitzel?
3. Name Jack's long-time announcer.
4. What was Rochester's last name?
5. How old did Jack claim to be?
6. What was Mary Livingstone's real name?
7. Jack had a long-time feud with what well-known comedian?
8. Name the two telephone operators.
9. Who was known as the silly kid?
10. Name Jack's first sponsor.

George Burns & Gracie Allen

Quiz #2

GEORGE BURNS & GRACIE ALLEN
(Answers on page 109)

1. Name George and Gracie's theme song.
2. What brand of coffee sponsored the show?
3. What is George's real name?
4. Before Gracie met George, what did she do in vaudeville?
5. Name the comedian who was George's best friend?
6. Who played The Happy Postman?
7. Who were the two announcers on the radio show?
8. Who was the announcer on the television show?
9. What did they both say at the end of the show?
10. George won the Academy Award for which movie?

George Burns & Jack Benny

Quiz #3

MATCH THE SAYING WITH THE PERSON
(Answers on Page 110)

1. "Hi yo, Silver. Away."
2. "On, you huskies."
3. "Gettum up, Scout."
4. "You ain't heard nothin' yet."
5. "I'm that man."
6. "That's a joke, son."
7. "So I ups to him"
8. "Good day."
9. "Leeeeeroy."
10. "Wonerful, wonderful."

a. Al Jolson
b. Paul Harvey
c. The Lone Ranger
d. The Great Gildersleeve
e. Sgt. Preston
f. Lawrence Welk
g. Tonto
h. Senator Claghorn
i. Matt Dillon
j. Jimmy Durante

8 The Old-Time Radio Trivia Book II

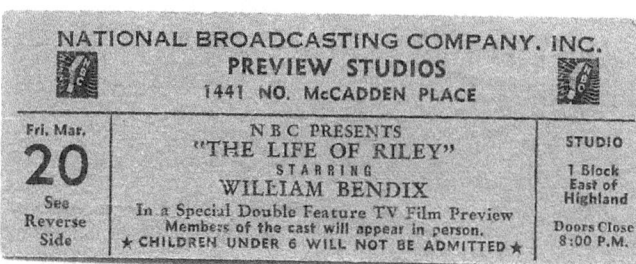

Tickets to radio shows

Quiz #4

SINGERS QUESTIONS
(Answers on Page 110)

1. Name the singer who was known as "The Voice."
2. Jo Stafford sang with which vocal group?
3. Who was the lead singer of The Andrews Sisters?
4. What famous singer was once married to Rita Hayworth?
5. Who was Frances Gumm?
6. Name the two singers who hosted the Kraft Music Hall.
7. What was the name of Mel Torme's vocal group?
8. Name the singer who was known as "The Songbird of the South."
9. Who was the lead singer of The Ink Spots?
10. Who was Benny Goodman's most famous female singer?

Marian & Jim Jordan, Fibber McGee & Molly

Quiz #5

FIBBER McGEE & MOLLY
(Answers on Page 110)

1. Where did Fibber and Molly live?
2. Name their long-time announcer.
3. What did Fibber call the announcer?
4. Who was their long-time sponsor?
5. Name the show's famous sound effect.
6. Who played Wallace Wimple?
7. What was his wife's name?
8. Molly played which character?
9. What did Gildersleeve do for a living?
10. Name the vocal group.

Don McNeil – The Breakfast Club

Quiz #6

MULTIPLE CHOICE
(Answers on Page 111)

1. Who was the host of *The Lux Radio Theater?*
   a) Cecil B. DeMille   b) William Keighley   c) Bert Parks

2. Who was the first host of *The CBS Mystery Theater?*
   a) Tammy Grimes   b) Stan Freberg   c) E. G. Marshall

3. Detective Mike Barnett was played by whom?
   a) Ralph Bellamy   b) Sidney Greenstreet   c) Peter Lorre

4. What did Johnny Dollar do for a living?
   a) Insurance investigator   b) Detective   c) Policeman

5. Name the two shows that Ovaltine sponsored.
   a) *Little Orphan Annie*   b) *Captain Marvel*   c) *Captain Midnight*

6. Which singer was known as "The Singing Lady"?
   a) Dinah Shore   b) Frances Langford   c) Irene Wicker

7. Who was Bing Crosby's announcer?
   a) Harlo Wilcox   b) Ken Carpenter   c) Don Wilson

8. Name the character that Mike Waring played.
   a) The Man In Black   b) The Falcon   c) The Mysterious Traveler

9. Who was known as "Radio's Bad Boy"?
   a) Henry Morgan   b) Walter Winchell   c) Jimmy Fidler

10. What were the last names of Vic & Sade?
    a) Smith   b) Jones   c) Gook

Eddie Cantor

Quiz #7

EDDIE CANTOR
(Answers on Page 111)

1. What was the name of Eddie's wife?
2. How many children did he have?
3. What was Eddie's nickname?
4. Name the character played by Bert Gordon.
5. What was always the character's opening sentence?
6. Name Eddie's theme song.
7. Who played Parkyakarkas?
8. Which radio quiz show did Eddie once host?
9. Name Eddie's last sponsor on radio.
10. Who played Eddie in the motion picture of his life?

Eddie Cantor and Al Jolson

Quiz #8

AL JOLSON
(Answers on Page 111)

1. Where was Al born?
2. Where did he grow up?
3. Name the year *The Jazz Singer* came out.
4. How many times was Al married?
5. Who was his most famous wife?
6. What was his biggest-selling record?
7. Who was his closest friend in show business?
8. What was his most famous radio show?
9. Who was his announcer?
10. Who was his orchestra leader?

Penny arcade cards

Quiz #9

TRUE OR FALSE
(Answers on Page 112)

1. *To Tell the Truth* was a popular radio show.
2. "Pops" was a nickname for Paul Whiteman.
3. *Sam 'n' Henry* was the original name for *Amos 'n' Andy*.
4. Don Cornell was a vocalist for Lawrence Welk.
5. Baron Munchausen was played by Joe Penner.
6. "Dizzy" Dean had a brother they called "Daffy."
7. Mel Allen did commercials for Schlitz beer.
8. Stoopnagle & Bud were a comedy team.
9. Bing Crosby was the first radio personality to record his show on audiotape.
10. Hopalong Cassidy's real name was William Boyd.

The Shadow

Quiz #10

THE SHADOW
(Answers on Page 112)

1. Who published *The Shadow* magazine?
2. *The Shadow* was on which network?
3. *The Shadow*, in reality, was who?
4. Name his lovely traveling companion.
5. Which day of the week was the program on?
6. Where did The Shadow learn to cloud man's minds?
7. Who was the Police Commissioner?
8. Name the long-time sponsor.
9. What was the name of the cab driver?
10. Who created *The Shadow?*

Quiz #11

GENERAL QUESTIONS
(Answers on Page 112)

1. Name the president who was known for his fireside chats.
2. Who was The Vagabond Lover?
3. What were Sam Spade's cases called?
4. What is a Lemac?
5. Jack, Doc, and Reggie were characters on which show?
6. Who was known as The Arkansas Traveler?
7. What musical instrument did Bob Burns invent?
8. Henry Morgan was a panelist on which television game show?
9. Name the long-time host of *The Metropolitan Opera*.
10. Who were The Happiness Boys?

Quiz #12

MATCH THE SAYING WITH THE PERSON
(Answers on Page 113)

1. "Here he is, the one, the only, Groucho."
2. "Heavenly Days"
3. "Oooooh, what's gonna happen to him?"
4. "This is London."
5. "Just the facts, ma'am."
6. "Good evening, anybody."
7. "Saints preserve us, Mr. Keen."
8. "Wait a minute. . .."
9. "Look out, Jerry. He's got a gun."
10. "Roll, thunder, roll."

a. Jack Benny
b. Edward R. Murrow
c. Sgt. Joe Friday
d. Molly McGee
e. George Fenneman
f. Red Ryder
g. Pamela North
h. Ralph Edwards
i. Henry Morgan
j. Mike Clancy

William Bendix, The Life of Riley

Quiz #13

THE LIFE OF RILEY
(Answers on Page 113)

1. Who preceded William Bendix as Riley?
2. What was Riley's first name?
3. Riley was married to whom?
4. How many children did he have?
5. What were their names?
6. What was the name of the friendly undertaker?
7. He was played by who?
8. What was his closing sentence?
9. Where did Riley work?
10. Who was the first television Riley?

Quiz #14

MATCH THE SPONSOR WITH THE SHOW
(Answers on Page 113)

1. The Lone Ranger
2. You Bet Your Life
3. Let's Pretend
4. Suspense
5. Amos 'n' Andy
6. Inner Sanctum
7. The Fat Man
8. The Life of Riley
9. Archie Andrews
10. The Green Hornet

a. Autolite
b. Bromo Seltzer
c. Cheerios
d. Orange Crush
e. Swift Foods
f. DeSoto-Plymouth
g. Pepto Bismol
h. Cream of Wheat
i. Rinso
j. Prell Shampoo

Quiz #15

SUPERMAN
(Answers on Page 114)

1. What was Superman's opening sentence as he was about to fly?
2. Who played Clark Kent and Superman?
3. Who was the long-time announcer?
4. Name the crime-fighting duo that often appeared on the show.
5. What character did Joan Alexander play?
6. Name the breakfast cereal that sponsored the show.
7. Who often said, "Great Caesar's ghost!"?
8. What did Clark Kent always say as he was about to change into Superman?
9. Who were Jerry Siegel and Joe Shuster?
10. Who played Superman on television?

The Andrew Sisters

Quiz #16

THE ANDREWS SISTERS
(Answers on Page 114)

1. What were their first names?
2. What was their hometown?
3. Name the bandleader who was their costar on *The Chesterfield Radio Show*.
4. Name their first record.
5. What was their biggest-selling record?
6. Name the comedian who wrote that song?
7. The sisters have the biggest-selling polka record ever. Name the polka.
8. What were the two hit records they had, which had the word apple in the title?
9. After she retired from singing, which sister taught speech drama in college?
10. Name the Broadway show that was based on their lives.

Guy Lombardo

Quiz #17

GUY LOMARDO
(Answers on Page 114)

1. Where was Guy Lombardo born?
2. What was his well-known theme song?
3. On his first radio show, his costars were who?
4. What was the band's catch phrase?
5. Name his three brothers who played in the band.
6. What was the name of the band?
7. For many years, the band ushered in which night of the year?
8. Guy's brother-in-law was the featured vocalist. Name him.
9. Guy won many awards for which sport?
10. What was his last radio show?

Quiz #18

MULTIPLE CHOICE
(Answers on Page 115)

1. The host of *Strike It Rich* was...
   a) Bill Cullen   b) Warren Hull   c) Phil Baker

2. *Lights Out* was written by...
   a) Ray Bradbury   b) Himan Brown   c) Arch Obler

3. Who was The Street Singer?
   a) Arthur Tracey   b) Jack Smith   c) Lanny Ross

4. Kraft Cheese is associated with which announcer?
   a) Harlo Wilcox   b) Ed Herlihy   c) Ken Roberts

5. Who became an Eagle Scout at the age of thirteen?
   a) Ozzie Nelson   b) Ezra Stone   c) Howard Duff

6. What was the name of Little Orphan Annie's dog?
   a) Fido   b) Butch   c) Sandy

7. William Gargan played which detective?
   a) Mr. Keen   b) Martin Kane   c) Pat Novak

8. What was Major Bowes's first name?
   a) Edward   b) Philip   c) John

9. "Kids Say the Darndest Things" was featured on which show?
   a) *Juvenile Jury*   b) *House Party*   c) *Let's Pretend*

10. Name the singer who has a degree in sociology.
    a) Dinah Shore   b) Tony Martin   c) Dorothy Collins

Quiz #19

VOCAL GROUPS THAT APPEARED ON RADIO
(Answers on Page 115)

1. Name the lead singer of The Ames Brothers.
2. Jo Stafford sang with which vocal group?
3. Who sang the song "Mr. Sandman"?
4. Name the McGuire Sisters.
5. Al Alberts sang with which group?
6. Perry Como recorded many songs with which vocal group?
7. Bing Crosby began his career singing with which group?
8. Name the lead singer of The Gaylords.
9. The Modernaires sang with which orchestra?
10. Who was the lead singer on *The Hoboken Four?*

Gum cards

Quiz #20

MATCH THE SAYING WITH THE PERSON
(Answers on Page 115)

1. "Call for Philip Morris!"
2. "I'm thinking it over."
3. "Thank you, music lovers."
4. "Who is buried in Grant's Tomb"?
5. "That ain't the way I heard it."
6. "Mr. Allen, Mr. Allen?"
7. "Heh, heh, heh… silly boy."
8. "That's My Friend Irma."
9. "I'm a bad boy."
10. "Hi, ho, everybody."

a. Groucho Marx
b. The Mad Russian
c. Rudy Vallee
d. Johnny
e. Jack Benny
f. Portland Hoffa
g. Lou Costello
h. Spike Jones
i. Jane Stacey
j. The Old Timer

Jimmy Durante

Quiz #21

JIMMY DURANTE
(Answers on Page 116)

1. What was Jimmy's nickname?
2. Which musical instrument did he play?
3. Name his famous vaudeville trio.
4. Who was Jimmy's straight man on radio?
5. Who said, "I'm feelin' mighty low"?
6. Name Jimmy's theme song.
7. What was always Jimmy's opening song?
8. Who did Jimmy always say goodnight to?
9. Name Jimmy's announcer.
10. What was Jimmy's last movie?

Quiz #22

COMEDIANS

From the following list of comedians: five appeared on radio, five appeared on television, five appeared on both.

(Answers on Page 116)

1. Milton Berle
2. Goodman Ace
3. Redd Foxx
4. Don Adams
5. Ed Wynn
6. Fred Allen
7. Fanny Brice
8. Dick Van Dyke
9. Phil Harris–Alice Faye
10. George Burns
11. Jack Pearl
12. Gertrude Berg
13. Bob Newhart
14. Carol Burnette
15. Joe Penner

Quiz #23

COMMERCIALS
Fill in the product
(Answers on Page 117)

1. Every kiss begins with _____.
2. _____ taste better, cleaner, fresher, smoother.
3. You know they're safe, you know they're safe, with _____ _____.
4. The pause that refreshes, _____ _____.
5. Which twin has the _____.
6. _____ Wines, made in California, for enjoyment throughout the world.
7. _____ Cards, when you care enough to send the very best.
8. Now you can be taller than she is. Get yourself a lift in _____ elevator shoes.
9. Who put eight great tomatoes in that little bitty can? _____ tomato paste.
10. The finest apples in apple land, make _____ apple juice just grand.

Walter Winchell

Quiz #24

WALTER WINCHELL
(Answers on Page 117)

1. Which newspaper did Walter write for?
2. Which night of the week was his radio show on?
3. Name his most popular radio show?
4. He began every show, saying what?
5. Name the bandleader that he had a friendly feud with.
6. Name the New York night club that he often visited.
7. For celebrities that he liked, he would award them with what?
8. Which singer punched and knocked Walter down in a night club?
9. Which two television personalities did he have a serious feud with?
10. Walter became the narrator for which television show?

Penny Singleton and Arthur Lake, Blondie

Penny Singleton, Blondie

Quiz #25

BLONDIE
(Answers on Page 117)

1. Who created the comic strip "Blondie"?
2. What was Blondie's last name?
3. Name Blondie's children.
4. What was the name of Dagwood's boss?
5. What was the name of the boss's wife?
6. Dagwood worked for which company?
7. Name Blondie's next-door neighbors.
8. What was the name of the mailman?
9. Who sponsored the show?
10. Name the rich lady that Dagwood was always bumping into.

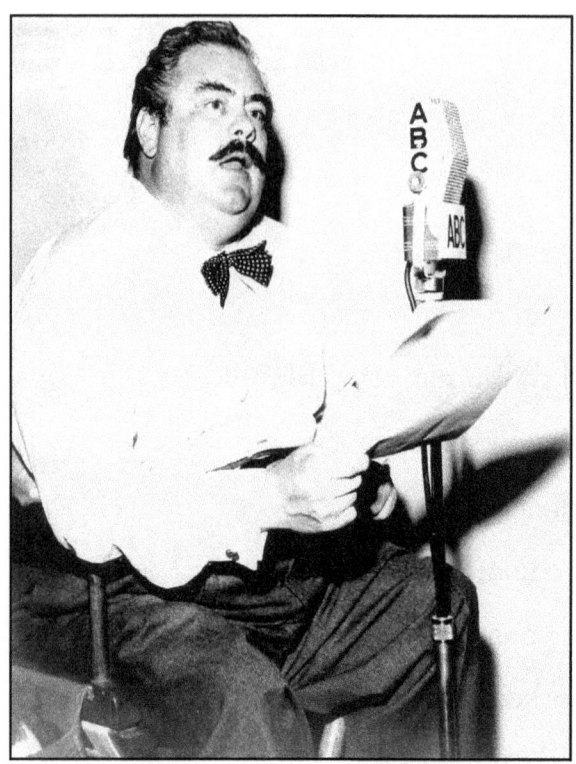

*J. Scott Smart,
The Fat Man*

*Julia Stevens –
The Romance of Helen
Trent/Vivian Smolen –
Our Gal Sunday*

Quiz #26

MATCH THE SOAP OPERA WITH THE STAR
(Answers on Page 118)

1. *The Romance of Helen Trent*
2. *Our Gal Sunday*
3. *Stella Dallas*
4. *Just Plain Bill*
5. *Pepper Young's Family*
6. *When a Girl Marries*
7. *Ma Perkins*
8. *Life Can Be Beautiful*
9. *Lorenzo Jones*
10. *Young Doctor Malone*

a. Virginia Payne
b. Mason Adams
c. Julie Stevens
d. Alice Reinheart
e. Anne Elsner
f. Arthur Hughes
g. Karl Swenson
h. Vivian Smolen
i. Sandy Becker
j. Mary Jane Higby

Marie Wilson, My Friend Irma

Quiz #27

MY FRIEND IRMA
(Answers on Page 118)

1. What was Irma's last name?
2. What did Irma do for a living?
3. Who was Irma's boyfriend?
4. How did he always greet Irma?
5. Name Irma's roommate.
6. Who created the show?
7. What did Mrs. O'Reilly do?
8. Who was the orchestra leader?
9. What was the show's theme song?
10. Who played Professor Kropotkin?

Arthur Godfrey

Quiz #28

ARTHUR GODFREY
(Answers on Page 118)

1. When Arthur Godfrey began his broadcasting career, what name did he use?
2. Which night of the week was the *Talent Scouts* show on?
3. When Godfrey fired Julius LaRosa, name the singer who replaced him?
4. Name his long-time announcer.
5. Who was Arthur's female singer from Ireland?
6. The singer who has had the most number one records in history, flunked an audition for the *Talent Scouts* show. Who was it?
7. What did Godfrey call his group of regulars?
8. Name his Hawaiian singer.
9. What was his biggest-selling record?
10. Which network was he associated with the longest?

Phil Harris and Alice Faye

Quiz #29

PHIL HARRIS — ALICE FAYE
(Answers on Page 119)

1. What was the original title of the *Phil Harris-Alice Faye Show?*
2. Which night of the week was it on?
3. Before Alice married Phil, who was she married to?
4. Alice began her career singing with whose band?
5. Who played the role of Frankie Remley?
6. What did Remley always call Phil?
7. What was the name of the delivery boy?
8. Name the actor who played him.
9. What was Phil's trademark song?
10. Phil had just one number one record. What was it?

Ed Gardner, Duffy's Tavern

Quiz #30

DUFFY'S TAVERN
(Answers on Page 119)

1. How often did Duffy appear on the show?
2. Ed Gardner was once married to which Academy Award-winning actress?
3. Who was the most famous person to play Miss Duffy?
4. Where did the show take place?
5. Name the show's theme song.
6. What was the name of Ed Gardner's character?
7. Who was his sidekick?
8. What was the name of the waiter?
9. Name the sound effect that began the show.
10. Name the television show that was a takeoff of *Duffy's Tavern*.

Penny arcade cards

Quiz #31

MULTIPLE CHOICE
(Answers on Page 119)

1. What was radio's first quiz show?
   a) *Information Please* b) *Dr. I. Q.* c) *Hobby Lobby*

2. Beula's boyfriend was whom?
   a) Robert b) Bill c) Arthur

3. The Signal Oil Company sponsored which show?
   a) *X Minus One* b) *The Whistler* c) *The Haunting Hour*

4. Frank Gallop was the announcer for which radio comedian?
   a) Jack Carson b) Ed Wynn c) Milton Berle

5. Radio station WGN is in which city?
   a) Boston b) Chicago c) St. Louis

6. Who had a popular Hollywood gossip show on radio?
   a) Hedda Hopper b) Jimmy Fidler c) Louella Parsons

7. Who lived at Melody Ranch?
   a) Tex Ritter b) The Cisco Kid c) Gene Autry

8. Who was Simon Templar?
   a) The Saint b) The Masked Tenor c) The Mysterious Traveler

9. Who played Aunt Fanny on *The Breakfast Club?*
   a) Fran Allison b) Cass Daily c) Canova

10. Abbott & Costello got their start on which radio show?
    a) Kate Smith b) Rudy Vallee c) Bing Crosby

Fred Allen

Quiz #32

FRED ALLEN
(Answers on Page 120)

1. Where was Fred born?
2. What was his real name?
3. What kind of an act did he do in vaudeville?
4. He was married to whom?
5. Who did he have a fun feud with on radio?
6. Name the sister vocal group.
7. What was his theme song?
8. Where did he spend his summer vacations?
9. Who played Senator Claghorn?
10. Minerva Pious played which character?

Freeman Gosden and Charles Corrall, Amos 'n' Andy

Quiz #33

AMOS 'N' ANDY
(Answers on Page 120)

1. What was the name of Amos's cab company?
2. Name the long-time announcer.
3. What was Andy's last name?
4. What was Amos's last name?
5. Who was Andy almost married to?
6. Name their theme song.
7. Name the lawyer on the show.
8. What was the name of the barber?
9. Who led the orchestra and chorus?
10. What was the name of Amos's wife?

Quiz #34

TRUE OR FALSE
(Answers on Page 120)

1. Snooky Lanson sang on radio's *Your Hit Parade.*
2. Mario Lanza once had his own radio show.
3. *Have Gun, Will Travel* began on television and then came to radio.
4. Aunt Fanny was a character on *The Sealtest Show.*
5. Bobby Benson's horse was named Flash.
6. Benny Goodman and Glen Miller were once roommates.
7. Corn Flakes sponsored *The Lone Ranger.*
8. Martin Block hosted *Make Believe Ballroom.*
9. The Colgate Sports Newsreel was hosted by Red Barber.
10. The leader of *The Harmonica Rascals* was Borrah Minevitch.

Quiz #35

MATCH THE HOOLYWOOD STAR WITH THE RADIO SHOW
(Answers on Page 121)

1. Basil Rathbone
2. Ronald Coleman
3. Vincent Price
4. Jean Hersholt
5. Jeff Chandler
6. Richard Widmark
7. Robert Young
8. Mickey Rooney
9. Frank Lovejoy
10. William Bendix

a. *The Halls of Ivy*
b. *Our Miss Brooks*
c. *Father Knows Best*
d. *The Life of Riley*
e. *Nightbeat*
f. *Sherlock Holmes*
g. *The Saint*
h. *Dr. Christian*
i. *Ethel & Albert*
j. *The Hardy Family*

Radio ads

Quiz #36

GENERAL QUESTIONS
(Answers on Page 121)

1. Who was the host of *Let's Pretend?*
2. How were Chick Carter and Nick Carter related?
3. Rosemary Clooney sang with what band?
4. Who was known as a wealthy young man about town?
5. The Mystery Melody was part of which show?
6. Who created *Inner Sanctum* and *Bulldog Drummond?*
7. What did Tom Mix call his young listeners?
8. Staats Cotsworth starred in which show?
9. Mr. Hush was featured on which show?
10. Who was known as the thief of bad gags?

Harold Peary, The Great Gildersleeve

Quiz #37

THE GREAT GILDERSLEEVE
(Answers on Page 121)

1. Gildersleeve got his start on which show?
2. What was his first name?
3. Name the town he lived in.
4. What did Gildy do for a living?
5. Name the southern belle who Gildy was once engaged to.
6. What role did Lillian Randolph play?
7. Gildy's niece Marjorie was married to whom?
8. Name the cheese company that sponsored the show.
9. What was the name of Gildy's singing group?
10. Who said, "Well, now, I wouldn't say that"?

Tommy Dorsey

Chesterfield Supper Club

Quiz #38

FILL IN THE SHOW
(Answers on Page 122)

1. Who knows what evil lurks in the hearts of men? ____ _____ knows.
2. I am _____ _____, and I know many things, for I walk by night.
3. I'm _____ _____. I live in a shoe.
4. Look! Up in the sky! It's a bird, it's a plane, it's _____.
5. Here comes _____ _____, your talent scout M.C.
6. We love the _____ _____ _____ that surround us here today.
7. So long to _____ _____ _____, and the tunes that you picked to be played. So long.
8. Champion of man and nature, _____ _____.
9. _____ _____ - enemy to those who make him an enemy, friend to those who have no friends.
10. A tale well calculated to keep you in _____.

Chesterfield Supper Club

Peg Lunch and Alan Bunce,
Ethel & Albert

Quiz #39

DETECTIVE SHOWS
From the following fifteen detective shows: five appeared on radio, five appeared on television, five appeared on both
(Answers on Page 122)

1. *The Fat Man*
2. *Richard Diamond*
3. *Dragnet*
4. *Cannon*
5. *Nick Carter*
6. *Kojak*
7. *Sam Spade*
8. *Mr. District Attorney*
9. *Hawaii-Five-O*
10. *Law & Order*
11. *Mr. Keen*
12. *Jake & The Fat Man*
13. *Boston Blackie*
14. *Mr. and Mrs. North*
15. *Mr. Chameleon*

Kate Smith

Quiz #40

KATE SMITH
(Answers on Page 123)

1. The majority of Kate's radio career was on which network?
2. Who was her manager?
3. Who was her announcer?
4. What was her theme song?
5. What was her biggest-selling record?
6. She introduced that song in which year?
7. Kate recorded for which record company?
8. She began her radio show saying what?
9. She closed her radio show saying what?
10. Name the hockey team she was associated with.

Jack Benny and Rochester

Quiz #41

MORE JACK BENNY
(Answers on Page 123)

1. Name Jack's longest-running sponsor.
2. What night of the week was the show on?
3. Who used to say, "Hiya Jackson!"?
4. What was the name of Mary's sister?
5. Who played Rochester?
6. Name the boys' club that Jack was a member of.
7. Sam Hearn played which character?
8. What was the name of Jack's bear?
9. Who made the sound of Jack's Maxwell?
10. Who used to say, "Hey, Bud. C'mere a minute"?

Jack Benny and Fred Allen

Quiz #42

MATCH THE THEME SONG WITH THE SHOW
(Answers on Page 123)

1. *Arthur Godfrey Time*
2. *The FBI In Peace and War*
3. *The Railroad Hour*
4. *You Bet Your Life*
5. *The Roy Rogers Show*
6. *Abie's Irish Rose*
7. *The Quiz Kids*
8. *Broadway Is My Beat*
9. *The Lives of Harry Lime*
10. *The Fred Waring Show*

a. "Happy Trails"
b. "My Wild Irish Rose"
c. "Seems Like Old Times"
d. "The Third Man Theme"
e. "I Hear Music"
f. "March from Love For Three Oranges"
g. "School Days"
h. "I've Been Working On the Railroad"
i. "I'll Take Manhattan"
j. "Hooray For Captain Spaulding"

Quiz #43

MUSICAL QUESTIONS
(Answers on Page 124)

1. Where was Benny Goodman born?
2. Who was the "Poet of the Piano"?
3. Name the singer who replaced Frank Sinatra when Frank left Tommy Dorsey?
4. What instrument did Xavier Cugat play?
5. Dinah Shore got her start on whose radio show?
6. Lucky Strike sponsored which musical radio show?
7. Who was Kay Kyser's girl singer?
8. What did Martin Block do on radio?
9. Singer Mel Torme appeared on his first radio show when he was four years old. Name the show.
10. Name the vocal group that consisted of Bing Crosby, Harry Barris, and Al Rinker.

Quiz #44

THE GREEN HORNET
(Answers on Page 124)

1. *The Green Hornet* came from which radio station?
2. What newspaper was Britt Reid the editor of?
3. Michael Axford did what for a living?
4. What was the Hornet's weapon of choice?
5. What nights of the week was the show on?
6. Who was the Green Hornet related to?
7. What did Britt Reid call his secretary?
8. How did the announcer begin the show?
9. Who created the show?
10. Name the soft drink that once sponsored the snow.

Cecil B. DeMille
First host the Lux Radio Theatre

Quiz #45

A DATE WITH JUDY AND *MEET CORLISS ARCHER*
(Answers on Page 124)

1. Both shows were female versions of which male radio character?
2. Who played Corliss Archer?
3. Who played Judy?
4. Name Judy's brother.
5. What was Judy's last name?
6. Who was Corliss's boyfriend?
7. Who was Judy's boyfriend?
8. Who played Judy's boyfriend?
9. Which role did Sam Edwards play?
10. Who played Corliss in the movies?

Quiz #46

TRUE OR FALSE
(Answers on Page 125)

1. Vincent Price was The Saint.
2. *Lassie* was once a radio show.
3. Elvis Presley once had his own radio show.
4. *Straight Arrow*'s horse was named Fury.
5. Kay Armen hosted *The Raleigh Room*.
6. Ronson sponsored *Twenty Questions*.
7. The Armchair Detective was Nero Wolfe.
8. The Friday night boxing bouts came from Madison Square Garden.
9. *I Love Lucy* was once on radio.
10. Jack Paar was once a summer replacement for Jack Benny.

Quiz #47

MATCH THE SINGER WITH THE BAND
(Answers on Page 125)

1. Bing Crosby
2. Bea Wain
3. Mike Douglas
4. Perry Como
5. Joe Williams
6. Rosemary Clooney
7. Merv Griffin
8. Ella Fitzgerald
9. Don Cornell
10. Doris Day

a. Count Basie
b. Tony Pastor
c. Paul Whiteman
d. Ted Weems
e. Les Brown
f. Larry Clinton
g. Sammy Kaye
h. Chick Webb
i. Kay Kyser
j. Freddy Martin

Brace Beemer, The Lone Ranger

Quiz #48

THE LONE RANGER
(Answers on Page 125)

1. Name the station that the show came from.
2. Where was the station located?
3. What was the name of the Lone Ranger's horse?
4. Tonto had two horses. Name them.
5. Who was the Lone Ranger's nephew?
6. What was the name of his horse?
7. Who created the show?
8. Name the famous theme song.
9. Who was their best-loved announcer?
10. Who was the Lone Ranger's biggest nemesis?

William Keighley
Second host of the Lux Radio Theatre

Quiz #49

FILL IN THE SHOW
(Answers on Page 126)

1. Waterman's Pens and Waterman's Ink presents _____.

2. The National Broadcasting Company, in cooperation with Galaxy Science Fiction Magazine, presents ____ _____ _____.

3. Uh-Uh-Uh-Uh. Don't touch that dial. Listen to _____.

4. Come on in. It's Art Linkletter's _____ _____.

5. Good morning, _____ _____, good morning to yah.

6. Tired of the everyday routine? Ever dream of a life of romantic adventure? Want to get away from it all? We offer you _____.

7. _____ _____ - Good evening, Mr. and Mrs. North and South America, and all the ships at sea.

8. America's favorite flying cowboy, _____ _____.

9. There he goes, into that drugstore. He's stepping on the scale. Weight 237 pounds. Fortune danger. Who is it? _____ _____ _____.

10. And now folks, get ready to smile again with radio's home folks, _____ _____ _____.

Bob Hastings, Archie Andrews

Quiz #50

ARCHIE ANDREWS
(Answers on Page 126)

1. Name Archie's high school.
2. Who was Archie's closest friend?
3. His closest friend was played by whom?
4. Name Archie's teacher.
5. Who was the principal?
6. Name Archie's two girlfriends.
7. What were the names of Archie's parents?
8. Archie's number-one rival was who?
9. Name the long-time sponsor.
10. This radio show was very similar to which other radio show?

Fanny Brice and Hanley Stafford, The Baby Snooks Show

Quiz #51

MATCH THE HOLLYWOOD STAR WITH THE RADIO SHOW
(Answers on Page 126)

1. Humphrey Bogart
2. Alan Ladd
3. Edward G. Robinson
4. Ralph Bellamy
5. Sydney Greenstreet
6. Bing Crosby
7. Groucho Marx
8. Orson Welles
9. Shirley Booth
10. Guy Madison

a. *You Bet Your Life*
b. *Duffy's Tavern*
c. *Kraft Music Hall*
d. *Box 13*
e. *The Lives of Harry Lime*
f. *Bold Venture*
g. *Big Town*
h. *Man Against Crime*
i. *Wild Bill Hickok*
j. *Nero Wolfe*

J. Carroll Naish, Life With Luigi

Quiz #52

LIFE WITH LUIGI
(Answers on Page 127)

1. What was Luigi's last name?
2. Name the city he lived in.
3. Who did he write a letter to every week?
4. What did he do for a living?
5. Who created the show?
6. What song did Luigi always sing?
7. Name the show's theme song.
8. Who was Luigi's landlord?
9. Name the landlord's daughter.
10. Who was Luigi's night-school teacher?

Quiz #53

GENERAL QUESTIONS
(Answers on Page 127)

1. Who created *Candid Microphone?*
2. Name the sportscaster who was known as "The Old Redhead."
3. What were the first names of the Bickersons?
4. Who was known as "The Robin Hood of the Old West"?
5. Name the leader of The NBC Symphony Orchestra.
6. Who was the host of *The Jergen's Journal?*
7. What does AFRS stand for?
8. Name the peanut butter that sponsored *Sky King*.
9. Who played Dr. Christian?
10. What state was Herb Shriner from?

Quiz #54

COMMERCIALS
Fill in the product:
(Answers on Page 127)

1. _____ Soap, ninety-nine and forty-four, one hundred percent pure. It floats.
2. Smoke dreams, from smoke rings, while a _____ burns.
3. With a name like _____, you know, you know it has to be good.
4. _____, the world's most honored watch.
5. Fly the friendly sky of _____.
6. I am stuck on _____ _____, and _____ _____ stuck on me.
7. _____ really stops B.O.!
8. I'd like to buy the world a _____.
9. _____, the soap for beautiful women.
10. Rely on _____.

Rudy Vallee

Quiz #55

RUDY VALLEE

(Answers on Page 128)

1. Name the state where Rudy was born.
2. Which college did he attend?
3. Rudy played which musical instrument?
4. What was the name of his first band?
5. What was his most successful radio show?
6. Name his theme song on radio.
7. What was the name of the nightclub that he owned in New York?
8. He was a bandleader in which branch of the service?
9. What was Rudy's biggest-selling record?
10. Rudy starred in which Broadway musical?

Rudy Vallee

Quiz #56

MATCH THE DOCTOR WITH THE SHOW
(Answers on Page 128)

1. Dr. Christian
2. Dr. I. Q.
3. Doc Gamble
4. Marcus Welby, M.D.
5. Dr. Kildare
6. Young Dr. Malone
7. Doc Adams
8. Dr. Sixgun
9. Doc Long
10. Dr. Watson

a. Sidekick to Sherlock Holmes
b. A character on *Gunsmoke*
c. Starred Lew Ayres
d. Appeared on *I Love a Mystery*
e. His first name was Jerry.
f. A popular quiz show
g. A character on *Fibber McGee & Molly*
h. Starred Jean Hersholt
i. Never was on radio, only television
j. Friend to white man and Indian

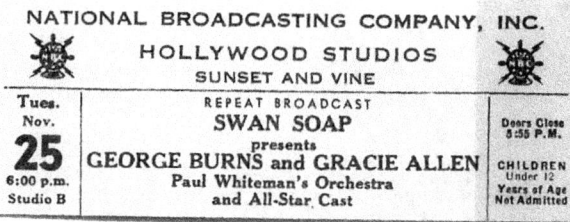

Tickets to Radio Shows

Quiz #57

MULTIPLE CHOICE
(Answers on Page 128)

1. Who lived in the little house halfway up the next block?
   a) Vic & Sade b) Myrt & Marge c) Lum & Abner

2. Who was the editor of *The Illustrated Press?*
   a) Perry White b) Steve Wilson c) Ed Asner

3. Which character did Tony Randall play in *I Love a Mystery?*
   a) Jack b) Doc c) Reggie

4. Who was The Answer Man?
   a) Garry Moore b) Albert Mitchell c) Clifton Fadiman

5. William Spier directed which radio show?
   a) *Escape* b) *The Haunted Hour* c) *Suspense*

6. Jeff Chandler played which detective?
   a) Michael Shayne b) Jeff Regan c) Nick Carter

7. What comedian was known as The Perfect Fool?
   a) Milton Berle b) Ed Wynn c) Bob Burns

8. William Paley was the head of which network?
   a) NBC b) CBS c) ABC

9. Who was the first radio star to record his show on audiotape?
   a) Al Jolson b) Bing Crosby c) Eddie Cantor

10. Which show did Ovaltine not sponsor?
    a) *Little Orphan Annie* b) *Captain Marvel* c) *Captain Midnight*

Gertrude Berg, The Goldbergs

Quiz #58

THE GOLDBERGS
(Answers on Page 129)

1. What was Mrs. Goldberg's first name?
2. What was her husband's name?
3. They had two children. Name them.
4. Where did the show take place?
5. Menasha Skulnik played which character?
6. Who wrote the show?
7. Who played Seymour Fingerhood?
8. Name the Goldbergs' next-door neighbor.
9. What did Mrs. Goldberg always yell when she called the neighbor?
10. Name the classical theme song of the show.

Quiz #59

GENERAL QUESTIONS
(Answers on Page 129)

1. Name the three McGuire Sisters.
2. Irving Cummings was the host of what show?
3. Who played Tom Mix on the radio?
4. What was the finest beer served anywhere?
5. Who was the champion of man and nature?
6. What does L-S-M-F-T stand for?
7. Colonel Stoopnagle's sidekick was who?
8. What was the last name of Vic and Sade?
9. Who was The Little Chatterbox?
10. Westbrook Van Voorhis was the host of which show?

Quiz #60

MATCH THE SAYING WITH THE PERSON
(Answers on Page 129)

1. "That's my dog, Tige. He lives in a shoe."
2. "Gotta clean out that closet one of these days."
3. "I got a million o' dem."
4. "Vas you dere, Sharlie?"
5. "So help me, I'll mow you down."
6. "Good night to you, and I do mean you."
7. "Pickle in dah middle and the mustard on top."
8. "You old goat."
9. "Stand by for news."
10. "Corrrrrrlissssss!"

a. The Great Gildersleeve
b. Jimmy Fidler
c. Jack Pearl
d. Fibber McGee
e. Buster Brown
f. Jimmy Durante
g. Dexter
h. Charlie McCarthy
i. Paul Harvey
j. Mr. Kitzel

Howdy Doody and Buffalo Bob Smith

Quiz #61

HOWDY DOODY
(Answers on Page 130)

1. When was the radio version of *Howdy Doody* on?
2. Who was the host of the show?
3. What instrument did he play?
4. Name the clown.
5. Who was the miserable old man?
6. He was the mayor of what city?
7. Name the Indian Princess.
8. She was played by whom?
9. Name Howdy's twin brother.
10. Name Howdy's twin sister.

Quiz #62

MUSICAL PROGRAMS
From the following list of musical programs: five appeared on radio, five appeared on television five appeared on both.
(Answers on Page 130)

1. *Your Hit Parade*
2. *American Bandstand*
3. *Sonny and Cher*
4. *The Andrews Sisters*
5. *Patty Page*
6. *Rudy Vallee*
7. *Bing Crosby*
8. *Sing Along With Mitch*
9. *Roberta Sherwood*
10. *Lanny Ross*
11. *Morton Downey*
12. *Grand Ole Opry*
13. *Arthur Tracy*
14. *Dennis Day*
15. *Andy Williams*

Quiz #63

GENERAL QUESTIONS
(Answers on Page 131)

1. Name Gene Autry's ranch.
2. Who played The Man In Black on *Suspense?*
3. Which comedian was known as The Perfect Fool?
4. The Sons of the Pioneers sang with which well-known cowboy?
5. Who was The Street Singer?
6. Name the detective that was the master of disguise.
7. What was the adjective that described Hildegarde?
8. Who said, "Thank you, music lovers"?
9. Tom Howard was the host of which show?
10. Victor Borge got his start on whose show?

ANSWERS

QUIZ #1 *(from page 3)*
1. "Love in Bloom"
2. Artie Auerbach
3. Don Wilson
4. Van Jones
5. 39
6. Sadie Marks
7. Fred Allen
8. Mabel & Gertrude
9. Dennis Day
10. Canada Dry

QUIZ #2 *(from page 5)*
1. "Love Nest"
2. Maxwell House Coffee
3. Nathan Birnbaum
4. She was a dancer.
5. Jack Benny
6. Mel Blanc
7. Harry Von Zell and Bill Goodwin
8. Harry Von Zell
9. George: "Say goodnight, Gracie."
    Gracie: "Good night, Gracie."
10. The Sunshine Boys

QUIZ #3 (from page 7)

1. c
2. e
3. g
4. a
5. i
6. h
7. j
8. b
9. d
10. f

QUIZ #4 (from page 9)

1. Frank Sinatra
2. The Pied Pipers
3. Patty
4. Dick Haymes
5. Judy Garland
6. Al Jolson and Bing Crosby
7. The Mel-Tones
8. Kate Smith
9. Bill Kenny
10. Peggy Lee

QUIZ #5 (from page 11)

1. 79 Wistful Vista
2. Harlow Wilcox
3. Waxey
4. Johnson's Wax
5. The opening of the hall closet
6. Bill Thompson
7. Sweetie Face
8. Teeny
9. He was a girdle salesman.
10. The Kings Men

QUIZ #6 (from page 13)
1. a and b
2. c
3. a
4. a
5. a and c
6. c
7. b
8. b
9. a
10. c

QUIZ #7 (from page 15)
1. Ida
2. Five
3. Banjo Eyes
4. The Mad Russian
5. How do you do?
6. "One Hour With You"
7. Harry Einstein
8. *Take It Or Leave It*
9. Pabst Blue Ribbon Beer
10. Keefe Brasselle

QUIZ #8 (from page 17)
1. St. Petersburg, Russia
2. Washington, D.C.
3. 1927
4. Four times
5. Ruby Keeler
6. "Sonny Boy"
7. Eddie Cantor
8. *Kraft Music Hall*
9. Ken Carpenter
10. Lou Bring

QUIZ #9   (from page 19)

1. False (It was only on television.)
2. True
3. True
4. False (He sang with Sammy Kaye.)
5. False (He was played by Jack Pearl.)
6. True
7. False (He did commercials for Ballantine.)
8. True
9. True
10. True

QUIZ #10   (from page 21)

1. Street and Smith
2. Mutual
3. Lamont Cranston
4. Margot Lane
5. Sunday
6. In the Orient
7. Commissioner Weston
8. Blue Coal
9. Shrevie
10. Walter Gibson

QUIZ #11   (from page 22)

1. Franklin D. Roosevelt
2. Rudy Vallee
3. Capers
4. Camel spelled backwards
5. *I Love a Mystery*
6. Bob Burns
7. The bazooka
8. *I've Got a Secret*
9. Milton Cross
10. Billy Jones and Ernie Hare

The Answers 113

QUIZ #12   *(from page 23)*
1. e
2. d
3. h
4. b
5. c
6. i
7. j
8. a
9. g
10. f

QUIZ #13   *(from page 25)*
1. Lionel Stander
2. Chester
3. Peg
4. Two
5. Babs and Junior
6. Digger O'Dell
7. John Brown
8. "Cheerio, I'd better be shoveling off!"
9. He worked in an aircraft plant.
10. Jackie Gleason

QUIZ #14   *(from page 26)*
1. c
2. f
3. h
4. a
5. i
6. b
7. g
8. j
9. e
10. d

QUIZ #15 *(from page 27)*

1. "Up, up, and away!"
2. Bud Collyer
3. Jackson Beck
4. Batman and Robin
5. Lois Lane
6. Kellogg's Pep
7. Perry White
8. "This looks like a job for Superman."
9. They created the *Superman* comic book
10. George Reeves

QUIZ #16 *(from page 29)*

1. LaVerne, Maxene, Patty
2. Minneapolis
3. Glen Miller
4. "Bei Mir Bist Du Schon"
5. "Rum and Coca Cola"
6. Morey Amsterdam
7. "Beer Barrell Polka"
8. "Apple Blossom Time" and "Don't Sit Under The Apple Tree"
9. Maxene
10. "Over Here"

QUIZ #17 *(from page 31)*

1. London, Ontario, Canada
2. "Auld Lang Syne"
3. George Burns and Gracie Allen
4. Sweetest music this side of heaven
5. Carmen, Lebert, Victor
6. The Royal Canadians
7. New Year's Eve
8. Kenny Gardner
9. Speed boat racing
10. *Your Hit Parade*

QUIZ #18 *(from page 32)*

1. b
2. c
3. a
4. b
5. a
6. c
7. b
8. a
9. b
10. a

QUIZ #19 *(from page 33)*

1. Ed Ames
2. The Pied Pipers
3. The Chordettes
4. Dorothy, Phyllis, Christine
5. The Four Aces
6. The Fontaine Sisters
7. The Rhythm Boys
8. Ronnie Gaylord
9. Glen Miller
10. Frank Sinatra

QUIZ #20 *(from page 35)*

1. d
2. e
3. h
4. a
5. j
6. f
7. b
8. i
9. g
10. c

QUIZ #21 *(from page 37)*
1. Schnozzola
2. Piano
3. Clayton, Jackson, and Durante
4. Garry Moore
5. Candy Candido
6. "Ink-a-Dink-a-Doo"
7. "Ya Gotta Start Off Each Day Wit' a Song"
8. Mrs. Calabash
9. Howard Petrie
10. *It's a Mad, Mad, Mad, Mad World*

QUIZ #22 *(from page 38)*
RADIO:
Goodman Ace
Phil Harris-Alice Faye
Joe Penner
Fanny Brice
Jack Pearl

TELEVISION:
Bob Newhart
Carol Burnette
Redd Foxx
Don Adams
Dick Van Dyke

BOTH:
Milton Berle
Gertrude Berg
Eddie Cantor
Fred Allen
Ed Wynn

QUIZ #23 *(from page 39)*

1. Kays
2. Luckies
3. Oil heat
4. Coca-Cola
5. Toni
6. Roma
7. Hallmark
8. Adler
9. Consadino
10. Motts

QUIZ #24 *(from page 41)*

1. *New York Daily Mirror*
2. Sunday
3. *Walter Winchell's Jergen's Journal*
4. "Good evening, Mr. and Mrs. North and South America, and all the ships at sea. Let's go to press."
5. Ben Bernie
6. The Stork Club
7. Orchids
8. Al Jolson
9. Ed Sullivan and Jack Paar
10. *The Untouchables*

QUIZ #25 *(from page 43)*

1. Chic Young
2. Bumstead
3. Cookie and Alexander
4. Mr. Dithers
5. Cora
6. J. C. Dithers Construction Company
7. Herb and Tootsie Woodley
8. Mr. Beasley
9. Super Suds
10. Mrs. Bufforington

QUIZ #26 (from page 45)
1. c
2. h
3. e
4. f
5. b
6. j
7. a
8. d
9. g
10. i

QUIZ #27 (from page 47)
1. Peterson
2. Secretary/stenographer
3. Al
4. "Hiya Chicken!"
5. Jane Stacy
6. Cy Howard
7. Irma's landlady
8. Lud Gluskin
9. "Friendship"
10. Hans Conried

QUIZ #28 (from page 49)
1. Red Godfrey
2. Monday
3. Pat Boone
4. Tony Marvin
5. Carmel Quinn
6. Elvis Presley
7. The Little Godfreys
8. Haleloke
9. "Too Fat Polka"
10. CBS

QUIZ #29 *(from page 51)*
1. *The Fitch Bandwagon*
2. Sunday
3. Tony Martin
4. Rudy Vallee
5. Elliott Lewis
6. Curley
7. Julius Abbruzio
8. Walter Tetley
9. "That's What I Like About the South"
10. "The Thing"

QUIZ #30 *(from page 53)*
1. Never
2. Shirley Booth
3. Shirley Booth
4. Third Avenue in New York City
5. "When Irish Eyes Are Smiling"
6. Archie
7. Finnegan
8. Eddie
9. Telephone ringing
10. *Cheers*

QUIZ #31 *(from page 55)*
1. a
2. b
3. b
4. c
5. b
6. all three
7. c
8. a
9. a
10. a

QUIZ #32 *(from page 57)*

1. Boston, Massachusetts
2. John Sullivan
3. He was a juggler.
4. Portland Hoffa
5. Jack Benny
6. The DeMarco Sisters
7. "Smile, Darn Ya, Smile"
8. Old Orchard, Maine
9. Kenny Delmar
10. Mrs. Nussbaum

QUIZ #33 *(from page 59)*

1. The Fresh Air Taxi Company
2. Bill Hay
3. Brown
4. Jones
5. Madame Queen
6. "The Perfect Song"
7. Algonquin J. Calhoun
8. Shorty
9. Jeff Alexander
10. Ruby

QUIZ #34 *(from page 60)*

1. False (He sang on the television version.)
2. True
3. True
4. False (She was on *The Breakfast Club*.)
5. False (The horse was named Fury.)
6. True
7. False (Cheerios was the sponsor.)
8. True
9. False (Bill Stern was the host.)
10. True

The Answers

QUIZ #35 *(from page 61)*
1. f
2. a
3. g
4. h
5. b
6. i
7. c
8. j
9. e
10. d

QUIZ #36 *(from page 63)*
1. Uncle Bill
2. Chick was the adopted son of Nick.
3. Tony Pastor
4. Lamont Cranston
5. *Stop the Music*
6. Himan Brown
7. Straight Shooters
8. *Casey, Crime Photographer*
9. *Truth or Consequences*
10. Milton Berle

QUIZ #37 *(from page 65)*
1. *Fibber McGee and Molly*
2. Throckmorton
3. Summerfield
4. Water Commissioner
5. Leila Ransom
6. Birdie, the maid
7. Bronco
8. Velveeta
9. The Jolly Boys
10. Peavey, the druggist

QUIZ #38 *(from page 67)*

1. The Shadow
2. The Whistler
3. Buster Brown
4. Superman
5. Arthur Godfrey
6. Halls of Ivy
7. Your Hit Parade
8. Mark Trail
9. Boston Blackie
10. Suspense

QUIZ #39 *(from page 69)*

RADIO
Mr. Keen
The Fat Man
Sam Spade
Mr. Chameleon
Nick Carter

TELEVISION
Cannon
Jake and the Fat Man
Law and Order
Hawaii-Five-O
Kojak

RADIO & TELEVISION
Mr. and Mrs. North
Richard Diamond
Boston Blackie
Dragnet
Mr. District Attorney

QUIZ #40 *(from page 71)*

1. CBS
2. Ted Collins
3. Ted Collins
4. "When the Moon Comes Over the Mountain"
5. "God Bless America"
6. 1938
7. Columbia Records
8. "Hello, everybody."
9. "Thanks for listening, and good night, folks."
10. The Philadelphia Flyers

QUIZ #41 *(from page 73)*

1. Lucky Strike
2. Sunday
3. Phil Harris
4. Babe
5. Eddie Anderson
6. Beverly Hills Beavers
7. Schlepperman
8. Carmichael
9. Mel Blanc
10. Sheldon Leonard

QUIZ #42 *(from page 75)*

1. c
2. f
3. h
4. j
5. a
6. b
7. g
8. i
9. d
10. e

QUIZ #43 *(from page 76)*

1. Chicago
2. Carmen Cavallaro
3. Dick Haymes
4. Violin
5. *Eddie Cantor Show*
6. *Your Hit Parade*
7. Ginny Simms
8. He was a disc jockey.
9. *Little Orphan Annie*
10. The Rhythm Boys

QUIZ #44 *(from page 77)*

1. WXYZ – Detroit
2. *The Daily Sentinel*
3. He was a reporter for the *Sentinel*.
4. The gas gun
5. Tuesday and Thursday
6. The Lone Ranger
7. Casey
8. "He hunts the biggest of all game…"
9. George W. Trendle
10. Orange Crush

QUIZ #45 *(from page 79)*

1. Henry Aldrich
2. Janet Waldo
3. Louise Erickson
4. Randolph
5. Foster
6. Dexter Franklin
7. Oogie Pringle
8. Richard Crenna
9. Judy's father
10. Shirley Temple

The Answers

QUIZ #46 *(from page 80)*

1. True
2. True
3. False
4. True
5. False (The hostess was Hildegarde.)
6. True
7. False (It was Ellery Queen.)
8. True
9. True
10. True

QUIZ #47 *(from page 81)*

1. c
2. f
3. i
4. d
5. a
6. b
7. j
8. h
9. g
10. e

QUIZ #48 *(from page 83)*

1. WXYZ
2. Detroit, Michigan
3. Silver
4. Paint and Scout
5. Dan Reid
6. Victor
7. George W. Trendle
8. "William Tell Overture"
9. Fred Foy
10. Butch Cavendish

QUIZ #49 (from page 85)
1. Gangbusters
2. X Minus One
3. Blondie
4. House Party
5. Breakfast Clubbers
6. Escape
7. Walter Winchell
8. Sky King
9. The Fat Man
10. Vic and Sade

QUIZ #50 (from page 87)
1. Riverdale High
2. Jughead
3. Harlen Stone
4. Miss Grundy
5. Mr. Weatherbee
6. Betty and Veronica
7. Mary and Fred
8. Reggie Mantle
9. Swift Meat Products
10. Henry Aldrich

QUIZ #51 (from page 89)
1. f
2. d
3. g
4. h
5. j
6. c
7. a
8. e
9. b
10. i

QUIZ #52 *(from page 91)*

1. Basco
2. Chicago
3. Mama Mia
4. He owned an antique store.
5. Cy Howard
6. "America, I Love You"
7. "Oh, Marie"
8. Pasquale
9. Rosa
10. Miss Spaulding

QUIZ #53 *(from page 92)*

1. Allen Funt
2. Red Barber
3. Blanche and John
4. The Cisco Kid
5. Arturo Toscanini
6. Walter Winchell
7. Armed Forces Radio Service
8. Peter Pan
9. Jean Hersholt
10. Indiana

QUIZ #54 *(from page 93)*

1. Ivory
2. Chesterfield
3. Smuckers
4. Helbrose
5. United
6. Band Aids
7. Lifebuoy
8. Coke
9. Camay
10. Spry

QUIZ #55 (from page 95)

1. Vermont
2. Yale
3. Saxophone
4. The Connecticut Yankees
5. *The Fleischmann Hour*
6. "My Time Is Your Time"
7. The Heigh-Ho Club
8. The Coast Guard
9. "The Maine Stein Song"
10. *How To Succeed In Business Without Really Trying*

QUIZ #56 (from page 97)

1. h
2. f
3. g
4. i
5. c
6. e
7. b
8. j
9. d
10. a

QUIZ #57 (from page 99)

1. a
2. b
3. c
4. b
5. c
6. a
7. b
8. b
9. b
10. b

QUIZ #58 (from page 101)
1. Molly
2. Jake
3. Rosalie and Sammy
4. The Bronx
5. Uncle David
6. Gertrude Berg
7. Arnold Stang
8. Mrs. Bloom
9. "Yoo-hoo! Is anybody…?"
10. "Toselli's Serenade"

QUIZ #59 (from page 102)
1. Phyllis, Dorothy, Christine
2. *Lux Radio Theater*
3. Curley Bradley
4. Pabst Blue Ribbon
5. Mark Trail
6. Lucky Strike means fine tobacco.
7. Bud
8. Gook
9. Little Orphan Annie
10. *The March of Time*

QUIZ #60 (from page 103)
1. e
2. d
3. f
4. c
5. h
6. b
7. j
8. a
9. i
10. g

QUIZ #61 *(from page 105)*

1. Saturday mornings
2. Buffalo Bob Smith
3. Piano
4. Clarabell
5. Phineas T. Bluster
6. Doodyville
7. Princess Summerfallwinterspring
8. Judy Tyler
9. Double Doody
10. Heidi Doody

QUIZ #62 *(from page 106)*

RADIO:
Rudy Vallee
Arthur Tracy
Lanny Ross
The Andrews Sisters
Morton Downey

TELEVISION:
Sing Along With Mitch
American Bandstand
Roberta Sherwood
Andy Williams
Sonny & Cher

BOTH:
Your Hit Parade
Kate Smith
Bing Crosby
Dennis Day
Grand Ole Opry

QUIZ #63 *(from page 107)*

1. Melody Ranch
2. Joseph Kearns
3. Ed Wynn
4. Roy Rogers
5. Arthur Tracy
6. Mr. Chameleon
7. Incomparable
8. Spike Jones
9. *It Pays To Be Ignorant*
10. Bing Crosby

www.ingramcontent.com/pod-product-compliance
Lightning Source LLC
Chambersburg PA
CBHW071449160426
43195CB00013B/2064